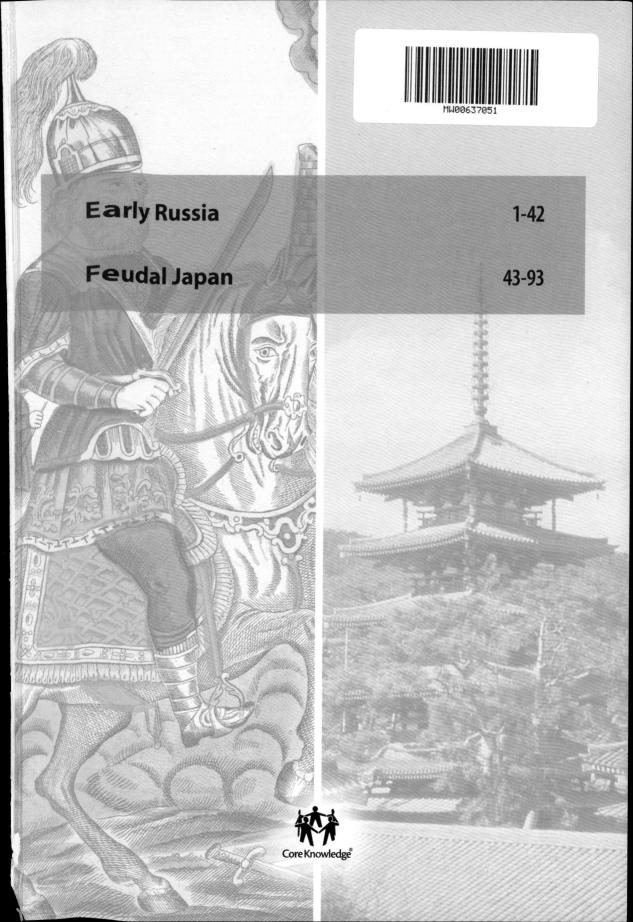

Core Knowledge®

ISBN: 978-1-68380-283-9

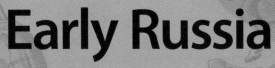

Early Russia

Table of Contents

Reader

Core Knowledge History and Geography™

Chapter 1
Russia's Beginnings

Meet the Giant Imagine a giant standing with his left foot in one world and his right in another. The giant takes a little from one world and a little from the other world, and tries to get along with both.

The Big Question

How did Russia become a Christian country?

That giant is the huge country of Russia, standing with one foot in Europe and the other in Asia. Russia is a big country. In fact, it is the biggest in the world. Russia is nearly twice the size of the United States.

Vocabulary

time zone, n. one of twenty-four zones around Earth within which everyone observes the same time

Russia is so wide that it stretches from Eastern Europe across northern Asia to the Pacific Ocean. It spans not only two continents, but also eleven **time zones**. That means someone living in western Russia is waking up in the morning just as someone living in eastern Russia is eating dinner in the evening.

ARCTIC OCEAN

1,000 miles

Kolyma River

Lena River

PACIFIC
OCEAN

China

Mongolia

SIBERIA

ASIA

Russia

Ob River

Ural Mountains

The Steppe

EUROPE

St. Petersburg

⭐ Moscow

Volga River

Caucasus
Mountains

Caspian Sea

Scandinavia

Kiev

Dnieper
River

Odessa

Black
Sea

N
W — E
S

180°E
160°E
140°E
120°E
100°E
80°E
60°E
40°E
0°E
40°N

Russia is a giant country that
crosses two continents.

3

As you learn about early Russia, you will read stories of high adventure, wars, weak rulers, and strong rulers. You will read about the growth of a mighty country from its humble beginnings in the early 800s to a great **empire** in the 1700s.

The Roots of Russia

Russia was not always as large as it is today. What we now call Russia first began as a series of small villages along the rivers in Eastern Europe. In the early years of the country's history, various groups of people spread throughout this area. Sometimes these people came to trade. Sometimes they came to conquer. But always they brought new ideas and customs. Among the earliest groups of people in Russia were the **Slavs**.

The Slavs probably came from the area of present-day eastern Poland, western Ukraine, and the Czech (/chek/) Republic. For the most part, these people were farmers. Some became merchants who traded with people in other countries. The Slavs spread throughout central Europe and Russia.

By 800 CE, the Slavs had built a number of towns along the rivers in southern Russia, including along the Dnieper (/dne*pur/) River. The Slavs used the rivers as trading routes. They developed contacts with many different groups of people and sometimes went to war against them.

The Vikings

As the Slavs were settling into the lands now called Russia, they collided with the Vikings, who were moving south from Scandinavia. Scandinavia includes the lands we now call Sweden, Norway, and Denmark. The Vikings are also called the Norse or the Norsemen. They were great warriors and traders.

As they pressed south, the Vikings sought trading partners. They wanted to trade their products from Scandinavia for products they did not make at home. Beginning in the 800s, the Vikings followed several of the long river routes into central Europe. These rivers carried Viking war and trading ships through the lands of the Slavs. The Slavs called the Vikings "Rus (/roos/)," a term for Swedish Vikings.

The Vikings liked the lands they explored on their voyages throughout central Europe and along the Dnieper River. The Dnieper River flows mainly through what is now Ukraine. Some Vikings decided to make their homes among the Slavs already living there. Many Slavs lived in what became the city of Kiev (/kee*ev/). You will read more about Kiev shortly.

The Vikings were more powerful than the Slavs. They forced the Slavs to trade with them, whether

The Vikings traded with the Slavs and eventually settled with them along the Dnieper River.

the Slavs wanted to or not. The Vikings often threatened the Slavs if the Slavs did not give the Vikings goods or money every year. This payment made by the Slavs to the more powerful Vikings was called **tribute**.

Over the years, however, the Slavic and Viking peoples blended together. They began to adopt each other's customs. They became the first people we call Russians today.

The Coming of Christianity

Another powerful influence on early Russia was Christianity. At the time of the Viking and Slav settlements, most Russians worshipped a variety of gods. As the Russians came into contact with other countries, they learned about religions such as Islam, Judaism, and Christianity. These religions teach that there is only one God.

Christianity worked its way into Russia from the Byzantine (/bihz*un*teen/) Empire, which was located to Russia's south. In the 800s, the Byzantine Empire was one of the most powerful empires in the world. Its capital was Constantinople. Greek **missionaries** from Constantinople brought Christianity to the Russian city of Kiev in about 900. The Byzantine form of Christianity was known as Orthodox Christianity.

These missionaries taught some of the early Russians about Christianity. One of these Russians was a princess named Olga, who lived in Kiev. Princess Olga was married to Igor I, the ruler of Kiev. After Igor was killed in 945, Olga took control of the

Constantinople was the capital of the very powerful Byzantine Empire.

government because her son was too young to rule. She was probably the first woman ruler in Russia.

A few years after she came to power, Olga traveled to Constantinople. While there, she met the Byzantine emperor. Supposedly, he was so struck by her beauty and wisdom that he asked her to marry him. She turned down the emperor's offer of marriage but asked him to teach her more about his religion.

Princess Olga of Kiev traveled to Constantinople, where she spent time learning about Orthodox Christianity.

The emperor wanted to please Princess Olga. He asked the patriarch (/pay*tree*ahrk/), or leader, of the Orthodox Church in Constantinople to teach her about Christianity. According to legend, Olga learned about Christianity "like a sponge absorbing water."

Olga then returned to Kiev and encouraged her people to practice Orthodox Christianity. Most Russians, however, stayed true to their old gods—the gods of nature, the winds, and the fields. Even Olga's son resisted her attempts to Christianize Kiev.

Years passed, and wooden statues of many different gods still stood in Kiev. Prince Vladimir, grandson of Princess Olga, ruled the city. Vladimir wanted Kiev to be a great power. He was interested in the religions of other great powers. He listened to traveling merchants who came to Kiev and spoke of religious beliefs in the Byzantine Empire and in Western Europe. Instead of many gods, the merchants spoke of a single, almighty God.

Prince Vladimir asked his **nobles** what they thought about other religions. They told him he should send "ten good and true men" to visit other lands to learn about other religions. In their visits, those men could

observe how people in other places worshipped. Prince Vladimir did as the nobles suggested. When the ten advisers returned, they reported that they were most impressed with Orthodox Christianity, and in particular with the magnificent Byzantine churches. The splendor and beauty of the churches took their breath away.

In 988, Vladimir became an Orthodox Christian, like his grandmother Princess Olga. He had the statues and pictures of the old gods and goddesses destroyed. Vladimir ordered all the people in Kiev to become Christians.

After converting to Orthodox Christianity, Vladimir forced all the people of Kiev to convert, too. It is said that Vladimir ordered that statues of Russian idols be thrown into the Dnieper River.

Chapter 2
The Mongols Invade

The Mongols "Give us trade," demanded the Vikings from the north. "Try our religion," urged missionaries from the south. Now a new voice was heard throughout Russia. "Pay us taxes," ordered the Mongols of the east.

The Big Question

What are some key features of Russian geography, and how have these features influenced the nation's history?

Because of its geography, Russia is a relatively easy country to invade from both east and west. It has suffered major invasions throughout its history. In the early 1200s, Russia endured one of the greatest and most important invasions in its history. The Mongols of central Asia invaded from the east.

Vocabulary

steppe, n. grassland plain

The invasion route into Russia from the east is especially easy. A grassland known as the **steppe** (/step/) stretches some five thousand miles from central Asia to Eastern Europe.

И шедшеп зжшаграбоуздаль . и цр̃ь
И коnpьстоуюбцьоуразграбьнша . ѽпро
чеасешгн҃і

мъпо

жҕ

The Mongols invaded Russia from the east. This image shows mounted archers attacking a Russian town.

ша

Most of the steppe is low and level grassland. The steppe has cold winters and hot, dry summers, much like the Great Plains of North America. Tribes of hard-riding warriors from central Asia have used the steppe as an invasion route into Russia and Eastern Europe for thousands of years.

Russia does have one important mountain range, the Urals. But the Urals are not very high mountains. Over the centuries, erosion has worn them down to mostly hills.

Mapmakers often use the Urals as a dividing line between Europe and Asia. Many geographers consider Russia west of the Urals as part of Europe and Russia east of the Urals as part of Asia. To be sure, the Urals make a better boundary than barrier. The Urals have never been high enough to block the movement of traders and warriors. In the 1200s, the Urals did little to stop the fierce Mongol invaders who galloped in from the Asian steppe.

Ferocious Conquerors

During the 1200s, the Mongols were one of the most powerful peoples in the world. They originated in central Asia and spread out in all directions. They conquered China and most of western Asia, as well as Russia. They created an enormous empire.

The Mongols were bloodthirsty warriors. They swept across Russia on horses specially trained to withstand the snow and cold. The Mongols were vicious in war. They would thunder into an area and destroy anyone or anything in their way. They left behind them a trail of dead bodies, burned villages, and ruined farmlands. People were terrified of the Mongols. A warning of their coming sent people running for a hiding place, but there were few places to hide.

The Mongol attack on Russia was especially destructive and deadly. In 1238, the Mongols charged into Russia and burned fourteen cities in a single month. Two years later, they attacked and burned Kiev. The Mongols killed most of the people and destroyed houses and buildings. Kiev was the most important city in Russia at that time. It would never again be as powerful as it was before the Mongol invasion.

The Mongol armies did not remain long in Russia. After they left, a group of people called the Tatars ruled Russia. The Tatars were a blend of Mongol and **Turkic** tribes. Turkic tribes had fought with the Mongols and remained in western Russia after the Mongols withdrew.

Vocabulary

Turkic, adj. related to one of the languages spoken in western and central Asia

The Beginnings of Moscow

Kiev had been losing power even before the Mongol invasions. Civil wars and raids by various nomadic tribes weakened the once powerful city, and fewer merchants came to trade there. As a result, the Russians in and around Kiev began to move to the northeast, where they built new farms, churches, and towns.

Moscow, one of these new settlements, rose from a small town into a key city. Located on **strategic** land and water trade routes, Moscow grew to become the most important center of a Russian state called Muscovy.

One ongoing problem prevented most of the Russian princes from growing even more powerful than they were. This was the problem of land ownership. When a Russian prince died, his sons split up his lands among themselves. Therefore, land holdings became smaller and smaller, and princes became weaker and weaker.

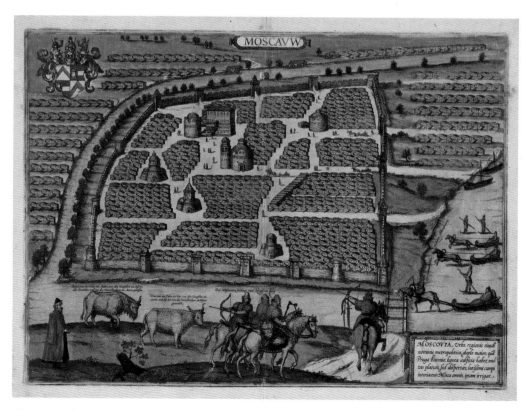

This map shows the Oka River, an important link that would help the development of Moscow as a major city.

In the city-state of Muscovy, land was not equally divided among the sons when a prince died. The oldest son received the largest share of land. Thus, Muscovy remained large while other city-states got smaller.

Muscovy had some very strong rulers during the early part of the 1300s. Among them was **Grand Prince** Ivan I. He remained on good terms with the Tatars mostly because he was very good at making sure people paid taxes. He was known for his tight control over financial matters and made himself very wealthy. He was so good at his job that he was nicknamed "Ivan the Moneybag."

Chapter 3
Ivan the Great

A Strong Ruler The next strong ruler of Muscovy was Ivan III, who became known as Ivan the Great. Ivan became Grand Prince of Muscovy in 1462 and ruled until 1502. He came into power at a time when Russian princes were still competing among themselves and struggling against the Tatars.

The Big Question

How did Ivan III gain more control over those he ruled?

No prince wanted power more dearly than Ivan III. He dedicated his entire life to making Muscovy the strongest state in Russia and to ridding his country of Tatar rule. No wonder he became known as Ivan the Great.

Ivan grew up in a period of almost continuous warfare. Often, this warfare took place among members of the same family. When Ivan was only a boy, some of his relatives rebelled against his father. They kidnapped his father and blinded him. Then they held him prisoner and tried to govern Muscovy themselves.

The Russians fought against the Tatars for many years.

With the help of some friends, young Ivan escaped capture, but not for long. One of the men who helped him escape later told the rebels where the young prince was hiding. The rebels found Ivan and carried him off. Ivan became a prisoner, like his father.

The struggle for control of Muscovy continued. Soon the supporters of Ivan and his father triumphed over the rebels. Ivan and his father were released, and they took power again.

At a young age, Ivan married the daughter of the then "Grand Prince." It was an arranged marriage, made for political reasons, not for love. Before he was twenty-two, Ivan led an army against his father's enemies and finally defeated them. He also fought against the Tatars. By the time his father died, Ivan had accomplished much. He was ready to take on the duties of Grand Prince of Muscovy. Ivan's father died in 1462, when Ivan was twenty-two years old. After that, Ivan ruled alone until 1502.

Winning Back Russia

As Ivan III gained power in Muscovy, there was conflict among the Tatar leaders in Russia. In 1480, a group of Russian princes led by Ivan III and his son forced the Tatars to retreat. Russia was at last free from foreign rule. Ivan took power into his own hands. Under his reign, and that of his son, the territories of Muscovy tripled in size. The Muscovy territories began to form a larger and more unified nation.

Ivan III copied the Tatar and Byzantine traditions of ruling with absolute power, a power no one could challenge.

As Ivan gained lands, he clamped down more tightly on all those he ruled. It became his mission to limit the power of the **boyars**, or landowning nobles. Ivan issued new, stricter laws. He punished anyone suspected of plotting against him with prison or death.

"Like God, the Highest"

Ivan III copied the Tatar and Byzantine traditions of ruling with absolute power—a power no one could challenge. Like the Byzantine emperors of the past, Ivan used the double-headed eagle as his symbol. In addition to his title of grand prince, he called

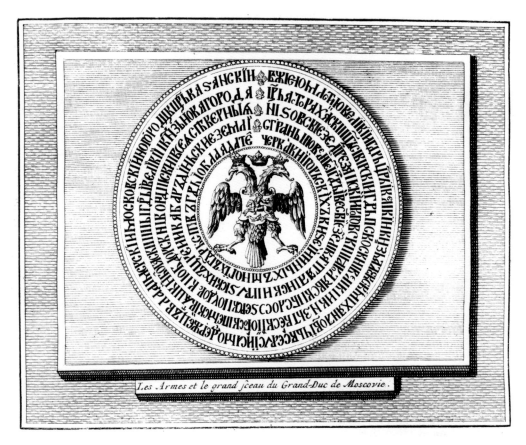

Ivan III used a double-headed eagle as his symbol.

himself **czar** or tsar, from the Russian word for "Caesar."

When Ivan became Grand Prince of Muscovy, great intellectual, artistic, and scientific progress was taking place in Western Europe. Historians call this period of history "the Renaissance." These great changes began in Italy and soon spread throughout Western Europe. But Russia was isolated, and the Renaissance had only a small impact on the country. Russia was mostly out of touch with the progress in the arts and sciences taking place in Western Europe.

There was one high-ranking person in Moscow who had firsthand knowledge of the changes taking place in Western Europe. That person was Ivan's second wife, Sophia. She had been raised in Italy and given a Renaissance education. But Sophia did not seem to have much influence on Ivan. She did not change him very much.

"The czar," Ivan was fond of saying, "is in nature like all men, but in authority, he is like God, the highest."

Ivan dressed as if he were, indeed, a god. He often appeared in robes woven from gold threads and lined with expensive fur. What a contrast this was to the tattered clothing and leaky boots of Russian workers and **serfs**.

The serfs were the millions of poor people in Russia who suffered under the harsh rule of the Russian princes and boyars. Most serfs were poor farmers. They farmed the land, did the hard work, and lived in miserable conditions.

When one landowner sold his farm to another, the serfs went with the sale. Some landowners also sold serfs individually, just like slaves. Serfs were not allowed to move from place to place without the consent of the landowner. Over the years, life for the serfs did not improve. In some ways the system of **serfdom** meant that things got worse for many people working on the land.

> **Vocabulary**
>
> **serf,** n. a peasant who is not free; a person living on a feudal estate who was required to work for the lord of the manor
>
> **serfdom,** n. an agricultural system in which people (serfs) were not free, but required to stay and work for a landowner as the owner demanded

Building His Reputation

Ivan III made up imaginary ancestors who just happened to be Roman emperors. He created legends about himself that showed him as glorious and strong.

To complete his image of greatness, Ivan started huge new building projects in the city of Moscow. Most large Russian cities had **kremlins**. The kremlins were built as walled fortresses to protect Russian cities. The rulers of a city usually lived inside the kremlins.

Кремль при Іоаннѣ III-мъ

While many Russian cities had kremlins, the Moscow Kremlin became the most important one. It was where the czar lived.

The czar lived in the Moscow Kremlin, which had been badly damaged by fire and needed repair. Ivan the Great changed that. He set about building many fine and grand structures inside the walls of the Moscow Kremlin. He built several very elaborate cathedrals, government buildings, and palaces. The newly rebuilt Moscow Kremlin stood as a grand symbol of Ivan's growing might and power.

Chapter 4
Ivan the Terrible

Fearful Times A storm shook Moscow on August 25, 1530, and as the thunder rolled, Ivan IV was born. According to legend, a **priest** had warned Ivan's father that he would have a wicked son. "Your states will be prey to terror and tears; rivers of blood will flow," the priest is supposed to have said. If he did say that, he was right.

The Big Question
....
Why was Ivan IV called "Ivan the Terrible"?

> **Vocabulary**
>
> **priest,** n. a person who has the training or authority to carry out certain religious ceremonies or rituals

The boy who was to become Ivan IV was a troubled, angry child. Unfortunately, for the Russian people, he became their czar. This grandson of Ivan the Great launched a reign of terror that earned him the reputation of being terrifying and eventually the title Ivan the Terrible.

When Ivan was three, his father died. Ivan became the Grand Prince of Muscovy, but he was only a child. The real ruling power rested in the hands of his mother, Yelena Glinskaya (/glin*sky*uh/), and the boyars who supported her.

Originally Ivan IV was known as Ivan the Terrifying, but over time he became known as Ivan the Terrible.

Yelena ruled for the next five years, receiving advice from relatives and boyars. Suddenly, one day she doubled over with pain and, within hours, she was dead. Some people believed that Ivan's mother had been poisoned.

Only eight years old, Ivan was alone in the world and still far too young to rule Muscovy. A power struggle broke out among the boyars for control over young Ivan.

As a young boy, Ivan probably felt afraid and uncertain. He spent his childhood being told he was a ruler, but for the most part, he was ignored. As the Grand Prince of Muscovy, Ivan lived in Moscow's Kremlin, where life was filled with violence as the nobles fought for power. He saw people unfairly arrested, exiled, and even killed, and he grew to distrust everyone around him.

A Czar Is Crowned

Ivan wanted to be crowned Czar of Russia. His grandfather, Ivan III, had claimed the title, but no Russian monarch had ever been crowned czar.

"Grand Prince" or "Czar"? It made little difference to the boyars. They agreed to his wishes. In Moscow on January 16, 1547, when he was not yet seventeen years old, Ivan was crowned Holy Czar, Monarch of All the Russians.

Czar Ivan IV was now ready to marry. According to tradition, boyars introduced their daughters to him. When Ivan saw Anastasia (/an*uh*sta*see*ya/) Romanovna (/roh*ma*nov*nah/), he offered her a jeweled handkerchief. He had found the woman he wanted to marry.

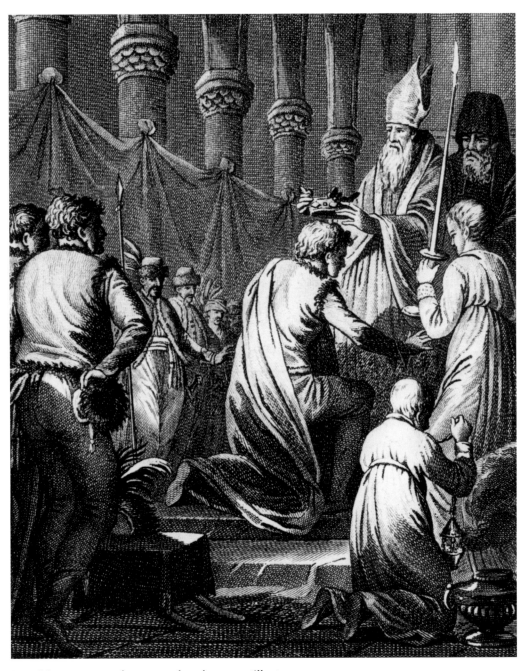

Ivan IV was crowned as czar when he was still a teenager.

Anastasia became Russia's **czarina**. She had a kind and gentle heart, and she cared deeply about the Russian people. Over the years, many lives were saved thanks to the czarina's gentle and calming influence on Ivan.

The Empire Builder

Ivan IV worked to expand his country's holdings to the east, including parts of Siberia, the largest part of present-day Russia.

Ivan IV built St. Basil's Cathedral in Moscow. The architect who worked on the cathedral with Ivan IV was from Italy.

In addition to parts of Siberia, Ivan added more lands to his territory by waging war with his neighbors to the south and west.

To celebrate one of his victories, Ivan built the beautiful onion-domed cathedral of St. Basil's in Moscow.

One legend says that Ivan asked the **architect** if he could ever build another church as fine as St. Basil's. When the architect said that he could, Ivan supposedly had the poor architect blinded to make sure he would not.

Spreading Terror

Ivan distrusted the boyars. He became more and more suspicious of them and began to suspect that enemies surrounded him. He began to **persecute** some of the boyars.

After giving birth to her sixth child, Czarina Anastasia became ill and died. The grieving czar fell into a sorrow that was close to madness. Once, in a fit of rage, he even struck and killed his favorite son.

As Ivan's temper grew worse, he became more vicious. He ordered arrests and executions. After a long, nasty reign, Ivan IV died in 1584 and left behind an empire of suffering, rebellious people. The years of disorder after Ivan's death became known as the Time of Troubles.

Chapter 5
Peter the Great

A New Dynasty In 1613 Mikhail (/mih*kuh*eel/) Romanov (/roh*muh*nawf/)—a relative of Czarina Anastasia Romanovna— was crowned czar. A young man

The Big Question
....
What did Peter the Great hope to do for Russia?

from a noble family, Mikhail restored order in Russia. His family, the Romanovs, would rule for more than three hundred years.

Czar Mikhail was eventually succeeded by two of his grandsons: Ivan and Peter, who were half brothers. Ivan was older and not as able as his younger brother Peter. Peter, who was born in 1672, had a quick mind and was very intelligent. The boys were crowned together and sat upon a special double throne. However, because they were still quite young, their older sister Sophia stepped in as ruler.

Young Peter

As a teenager, Peter explored Moscow's German Quarter, the section of town where Moscow's Germans and other foreigners lived. Its residents wore Western European clothes and ate Western European food. Their Western ways fascinated Peter.

In 1613, Mikhail Romanov was crowned czar of Russia.

By age twenty-three, Peter was a man who towered over his **subjects** in every way. In his boots, he stood nearly seven feet tall, which would be considered very tall even by today's standards. Back in 1695, he was such an unusually tall man that people sometimes called him "Peter the Giant."

Eventually, his sister was overthrown, his half brother died, and Peter **reigned** alone. Czar Peter set out to make Russia a modern European nation.

The Traveling Czar

In 1697, Peter began a lengthy tour of Western Europe. He planned to travel in disguise, but it was difficult to disguise a nearly seven-foot czar. Peter brought home chests filled with weapons and scientific tools. He even brought home a stuffed crocodile. He also returned to Russia with a group of European engineers, soldiers, and scientists who would teach their skills to his people. Two barbers were among Peter's group of Europeans. The czar had decided that his noblemen should get rid of their old-fashioned, long Russian-style beards.

"Shave off your beards . . . or else," Peter ordered, and his order became the law of the land. Any upper-class Russian who wanted to wear a beard had to pay a beard tax. Then, and only then, would he be allowed to keep his whiskers.

Peter used his power as czar to put his new ideas into action. He replaced the old Russian calendar with the newer European calendar—the Gregorian Calendar—which numbered the years from the birth of Jesus. He had engineers design canals to link Russian rivers, and he had instructors teach Russians mathematics and navigation.

Peter did modernize Russia, but not all aspects of Russian life moved forward. Even under Peter's rule, the serfs

Under Peter the Great's orders, Russian noblemen had to have their beards cut off or pay a beard tax.

continued to live in terrible poverty. As a result, the gap between Russia and Western Europe widened. Serfdom had died out in Western Europe. In Russia, it spread. As Russia expanded, more and more serfs spent their entire lives working the land and paying taxes to landowners. Others labored long hours building roads and canals. Unlike some of the poor farmers in Western Europe who were enjoying new freedoms, Russia's serfs remained controlled by landowners and had no freedoms.

Seeking a Warm-Water Port

While Peter made many changes in Russia, he could do nothing to change its geography. Russia's first seaports were on the Baltic Sea and the Arctic Ocean. If you look at a map of Russia, you will find that these large bodies of water are located along the northern coast of the country. In winter, they are choked with ice.

As a result, early Russia was a country bordered by oceans that froze in the winter. For centuries, Russian rulers had fought bloody wars to gain a **warm-water port** where they could trade year-round. They especially wanted a port on the Black Sea, but their efforts had been unsuccessful. Peter the Great also tried to gain a warm-water port for Russian trade, but at this he failed.

> ## Vocabulary
>
> **"warm-water port,"** (phrase), a port with waters that do not freeze during the winter; ships can use a warm-water port all year long
>
> **marsh,** n. an area of waterlogged land, usually overgrown with tall grasses; a swamp

Window on the West

Czar Peter did succeed in building a city. Peter found Moscow a gloomy place. He decided to build the city of St. Petersburg and make it his capital. He hired French and Italian architects to help him plan and build a city that had grand structures like the ones found in the major cities of Western Europe—Paris, Amsterdam, and London.

Peter chose a swampy site near the Baltic Sea for his new city. When serfs were forced to drain the **marshes**, thousands fell ill and died. People began to call St. Petersburg the "city built on bones."

Many of the nobles did not want to leave Moscow, but Peter ordered them to build costly homes in St. Petersburg. He was sure this new city, which he called his "window on the West" would establish Russia as a European power. More than anything, Peter

The Winter Palace in St. Petersburg was built in the style of Western architecture of the time.

wanted Russia to look westward and to align itself with the nations and culture of Western Europe. He feared that a lack of progress would weaken Russia in the political world.

A Great Title

In his last years as czar, Peter signed a treaty with Sweden that protected the lands around St. Petersburg. To celebrate, Peter decided to call himself "Peter the Great, Emperor of Russia."

By the time he was fifty-two years old, illness had drained Peter's energy. One winter's day he waded into the icy sea to rescue some fishermen. He saved the men, but it took all his strength. On January 28, 1725, Czar Peter died.

Chapter 6
Catherine the Great

A German Princess Following the death of Peter the Great in 1725, a series of weak rulers governed Russia for thirty-seven years. Toward the end of this period, a dynamic young woman from Germany became a part of Russian history.

The Big Question

Why did serfdom continue in Russia?

Vocabulary

principality, n. a small territory or land usually ruled by a prince

Picture this situation: In a small **principality** in Germany, the ruler asked his fifteen-year-old daughter, "What do you think, Sophia? How would you like to marry a Russian grand duke?"

Young Sophia considered the offer. After all, this particular grand duke, Peter III, was in line to become Russia's czar. It would be a good match for an ambitious German princess, even if Peter was rumored to be a bit of a fool and far from handsome. "Well," thought Sophia, "as grand duchess, I might sooner or later rise to power myself."

Catherine the Great was born a German princess but became one of Russia's greatest rulers.

The princess traveled to Russia to meet the sixteen-year-old grand duke. Peter, who had spent much of his life in Germany, was willing to marry the girl chosen for him. Before the wedding in 1744, Sophia converted to the Russian Orthodox religion. She also took a new name, Catherine.

As grand duchess, Catherine learned Russian and made many new friends. She was, however, less pleased with her husband. Peter seemed young for his age and uninterested in his bride. It is said that he liked to play with toy soldiers.

Catherine Takes the Crown

As expected, Peter inherited the throne of Russia. Czar Peter III made few friends and many enemies. Some of his royal orders were just plain silly. One of his laws allowed nobles to hunt in the streets of St. Petersburg. Finally, he went too far. He threatened to involve Russia in a war against Denmark. His enemies sprang into action. They planned to replace Peter with his capable wife.

Catherine agreed to the overthrow of her husband, and Peter was soon arrested. A few days after Peter's arrest, Catherine received a note saying that her husband was dead. He had been murdered. It is unclear whether Catherine had a role in his death, but his death was her path to the throne.

At age thirty-three, Catherine became an empress—a crowned ruler with absolute power. Like Peter the Great, Catherine admired Western Europe. She read many books by French writers that filled her mind with new ideas. She asked her nobles to speak French and to adopt French styles.

Catherine, following in Peter the Great's footsteps, put people to work. She made officials find ways to improve roads and rebuild towns and cities. She offered free education for some Russian boys and girls. However, free education was not offered to the children of Russia's serfs. Since the serfs made up the vast majority of the population, most boys and girls in Russia did not receive an education.

After the death of her husband, Catherine was crowned empress of Russia. Catherine's crown has five thousand diamonds and two rows of pearls. The diamonds are arranged in a tree branch and wreath pattern.

No Change for the Serfs

Although she was intelligent and forward thinking, Catherine, like Peter the Great, continued to support serfdom. Actually, Catherine did study the idea of freeing Russia's serfs, but she decided against it. She feared that the end of serfdom would weaken her country and displease the nobles. In fact, the number of serfs actually increased as Catherine's empire grew. She even *donated* hundreds of thousands of serfs to various noblemen as rewards for their loyalty and service. Life became harder for the serfs during Catherine's reign.

For more than three centuries, Russia's serfs were almost like enslaved people under the control of Russian nobles.

As long as serfdom was linked to the creation of wealth and a successful economy, it would not be easily reformed or abandoned. Likewise, other countries were struggling with the idea of slavery. Southern plantation owners in the British colonies of North America would not even consider freeing their enslaved workers. They, too, saw slave labor as an essential part of a growing economy. So it is not surprising that Catherine the Great could not see a way for Russia to free its serfs.

A Stronger Russia

Catherine shared Peter the Great's goal of gaining a warm-water port. After a war against the Turks, Catherine achieved that goal. She conquered the northern shore of the Black Sea and built a

The painting shows the Russians capturing a Turkish fortress during the Russo-Turkish War (1787–1792).

warm-water port called Odessa. The treaty of peace with the Turks gave Russian ships on the Black Sea free passage through the narrow strip of Turkish-controlled water between the Black Sea and the Mediterranean. At last, Russian ships could sail and trade when northern seas were frozen.

In 1796, Catherine died at the age of sixty-seven. Even the last years of her life had been active ones. She set up a fur-trading colony in Alaska and continued to run her government.

Fifty-two years had passed since the young German princess dreamed of power and glory. In some ways, she did not do much to help her people. Most of her subjects, the serfs, remained little more than enslaved workers. Yet in other ways, she brought Russia into the future by building roads and schools, and by securing the warm-water port Russian czars had been seeking for hundreds of years.

Glossary

A

architect, n. a person who designs buildings **(29)**

B

boyar, n. a rich landowner in medieval Russia **(19)**

C

czar, n. from the word "Caesar," the title of an emperor of Russia before 1917; sometimes spelled tsar **(20)**

czarina, n. the wife of a czar **(27)**

E

empire, n. a group of countries or territories under the control of one government or one ruler **(4)**

G

"Grand Prince," (phrase), mainly Russian, the leader of all the people and head of the government of a city-state or region **(15)**

K

kremlin, n. a central fortress built to protect a Russian city; today the term generally refers to the fortress in central Moscow **(22)**

M

marsh, n. an area of waterlogged land, usually overgrown with tall grasses; a swamp **(34)**

missionary, n. a person on a journey for the purpose of spreading a particular religious belief **(6)**

N

noble, n. a person who belongs to the highest social class of a country **(9)**

P

persecute, n. to treat people cruelly and unfairly **(29)**

priest, n. a person who has the training or authority to carry out certain religious ceremonies or rituals **(24)**

principality, n. a small territory or land usually ruled by a prince **(36)**

R

reign, v. to rule over a country as its czar, king, or queen **(32)**

S

serf, n. a peasant who is not free; a person living on a feudal estate who was required to work for the lord of the manor **(21)**

serfdom, n. an agricultural system in which people (serfs) were not free, but required to stay and work for a landowner as the owner demanded **(21)**

Slav, n. a person who belongs to an ethnic group of people that settled in Eastern Europe many years ago; the Slavs include Russians, Ukrainians, Poles, and Czechs. **(4)**

steppe, n. grassland plain **(10)**

strategic, adj. useful or important to achieving a goal or completing a plan, especially in a war **(14)**

subject, n. a person governed by the laws of a czar, king, or queen **(32)**

T

time zone, n. one of twenty-four zones around Earth within which everyone observes the same time **(2)**

tribute, n. payment of money or goods by a people or their ruler to another country or ruler in exchange for protection **(6)**

Turkic, adj. related to one of the languages spoken in western and central Asia **(13)**

W

"warm-water port," (phrase), a port with waters that do not freeze during the winter; ships can use a warm-water port all year long **(34)**

Feudal Japan

Table of Contents

Reader

Core Knowledge History and Geography™

Chapter 1
The Rise of an Empire

Japan, Now and Then Japan is an island nation in the Pacific Ocean. It is located east of China and the Korean Peninsula, and is part of what we call the **Pacific Rim**. To people in these lands, the sun seems to rise first over Japan. That is probably why the Japanese call their country Nippon, which means origin of the sun.

The Big Question

How did China and Korea influence the development of Japanese culture?

Vocabulary

Pacific Rim, n. a term used to describe nations that border the Pacific Ocean

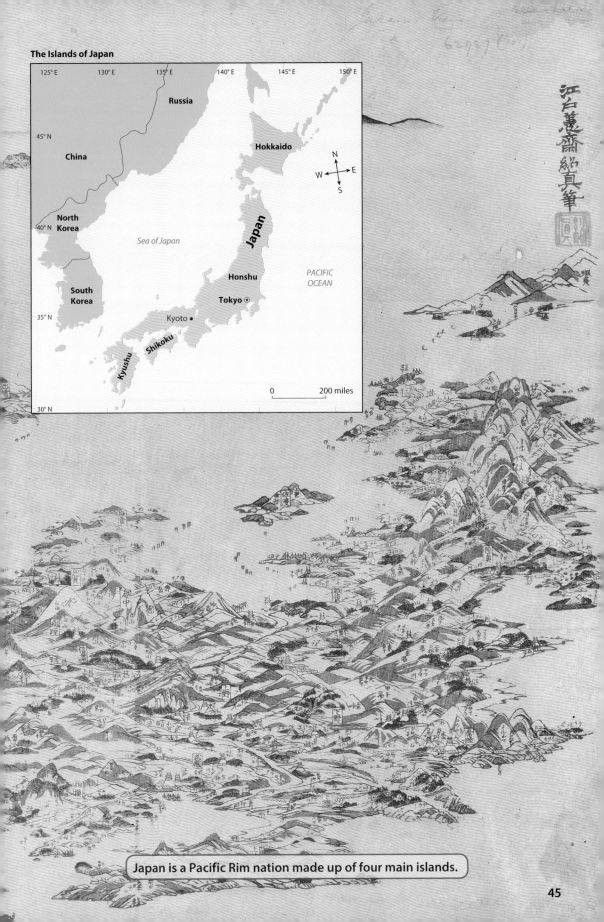

The Islands of Japan

Russia

China

North Korea

South Korea

Hokkaido

Sea of Japan

Japan

Honshu

Tokyo ⊛

Kyoto •

Kyushu

Shikoku

PACIFIC OCEAN

N
W — E
S

0   200 miles

Japan is a Pacific Rim nation made up of four main islands.

There are four major islands and thousands of small ones in the Japanese **archipelago** (/ar*kuh*peh*luh*goh/). The largest island is Honshu (/hahn*shoo/), the home of the capital city of Tokyo (/toh*kee*oh/), Kyoto (/kee*yoh*toh/), and other great cities. To the south lie the major islands of Shikoku (/shih*koh*koo/) and Kyushu (/kee*yoo*shoo/), and to the north is Hokkaido (/hah*kye*doh/).

Today these islands make up one of the most economically advanced nations in the world. Japanese companies ship automobiles and electronic goods all over the world, and hundreds of thousands of travelers fly in and out of Tokyo's busy airports every day. But Japan was not always so open to foreigners. For several centuries, Japan distrusted outsiders and lived in self-imposed **isolation**. At various times in their history, the Japanese were deeply influenced by their near neighbors—the Koreans and the Chinese. But they shut their doors almost completely to Europeans and Americans between the 1600s and the mid-1800s.

History and Legends

Throughout much of their early history, the Japanese lived in social groups of families and friends called **clans**. Each clan had its own chief. It also worshipped one god or goddess as its ancestor— its link to heaven.

In about 400 CE, the Yamato (/yah*mah*toh/) clan, which lived on the central island of Honshu, became the strongest of the clans. The Yamatos identified themselves as descendants of the goddess Amaterasu (/ah*mah*ter*ah*soo/) and declared their right to rule Japan.

The Legend of Amaterasu

The Yamatos supported their claim to the throne with a mystical legend. According to this legend, a god and goddess were strolling on the rainbow bridge that led from the sky to the dark sea below. They dipped a jeweled spear into the ocean and shook it into the sky. Drops of sea spray became the first island of Japan. The goddess then gave birth to the rest of the islands.

The godly pair created children to help rule the islands. One was Amaterasu, goddess of the sun, who lived in the sky. As time passed, Amaterasu bore

According to legend, the first emperors of Japan were related to Amaterasu, the goddess of the sun.

many gods and goddesses. Among her first children was one man. He became Japan's first emperor.

In 645 CE, because of his family's power and the legend of Amaterasu, the head of the Yamato clan became emperor of Japan. He called himself the son of heaven and chose the rising sun as the symbol of his empire. For centuries, the Japanese honored their emperors as living gods. Today's emperor still traces his roots to the Yamato clan.

Borrowing from Neighbors

During this early period of Japanese history, the Japanese borrowed or were inspired by certain things that came from Korea or from China. It appears that the early Japanese had no written language. Inspired by China's writing system, the Japanese used simplified forms of Chinese characters to create a writing system of their own. Korean craftsmen taught the Japanese to make tools and ornaments of bronze and iron.

However, the Korean import that had the greatest effect on Japan was a new religion. The Japanese had long practiced a nature religion known as **Shinto**. In about 550 CE, the Koreans introduced a Chinese form of **Buddhism**.

One day a Korean boat dropped anchor on the Japanese shore. Korean sailors moved a large box down the **gangplank**. A gong sounded. Priests chanted as a gold and copper statue of Buddha was lifted from the box and displayed to the people.

> ### Vocabulary
>
> **Shinto**, n. a Japanese religion in which people worship gods and spirits associated with nature
>
> **Buddhism**, n. a religion that began in India and is based on the teachings of Siddhartha Gautama
>
> **gangplank**, n. a small movable bridge used to get on and off a ship

The new religion spread slowly, but eventually it took root in Japan. The ceremonies of Buddhism with the gongs, priestly robes, and candlelit altars attracted many Japanese. The religion itself attracted many people, as Buddhism promotes the personal search for a state of peacefulness, without suffering. The new religion also increased Japan's fascination with mainland culture and especially with all things Chinese.

In the 600s, Prince Shotoku (/sho*toh*koo/), a powerful Yamato prince, became fascinated with China. He realized that much of what the Japanese had learned from the Koreans was actually coming from China. Instead of learning about Chinese ideas indirectly, through the Koreans, the emperor decided to go directly to the source. He sent young Japanese nobles to China to study its culture.

After this expedition, Chinese ways became examples to follow. The Japanese built their first capital city at Nara, laid out like the capital of China. Japanese nobles began dressing in Chinese fashions. The Japanese studied Chinese philosophies, literature, geography, medicine, and astronomy. They imitated Chinese patterns of government and adopted the Chinese calendar. They imported the custom of tea drinking and created elaborate **tea ceremonies**. They even learned to raise **silkworms** and weave silk.

> ### Vocabulary
>
> **tea ceremony,** n. a way of preparing and presenting tea
>
> **silkworm,** n. a caterpillar that produces silk, which is used to make thread or cloth

This temple in the city of Nara, Japan, was built in 607 CE.

Japanese Culture

All of these imported ideas helped Japan grow stronger. Eventually, the country no longer felt the need to rely so heavily on its mainland neighbors. After the 800s, the Japanese changed some Chinese ways to suit Japanese needs and styles. For instance, instead of choosing government officials based on tests of ability, as the Chinese had done, the Japanese decided to fill the government positions with the sons of Japanese nobles. This meant that **aristocrats** controlled the government.

There were cultural changes as well. Japanese artists added color to the traditional black ink of Chinese paintings. They wrote their own poems and sculpted in bronze. Wealthy landowners supported artists and encouraged a Japanese style. All of these changes led to the development of a unique Japanese culture.

Japanese bronze statue

Chapter 2
Religion in Japan

Native and Imported Religions

Two of the religions that have helped shape the Japanese people are Shinto and Buddhism. Shinto is the native religion. Buddhism is the faith that Korean missionaries brought from China.

The Big Question

What are the basic teachings of the Shinto and Buddhist religions?

Shinto: Spirits in Nature

Shinto is Japan's oldest religion. It is based on nature. Japan is a land of pine forests, oceans, and green rice fields. It is the place where snowcapped Fuji, the country's tallest mountain, rises high into the clouds. From the earliest times, Japan's people have celebrated their country in poetry and art. This love of nature is at the heart of Shinto.

Vocabulary

spirit, n. an unseen life-giving force

Followers of Shinto believe that each part of nature contains a **spirit**. These spirits are known as kami (/kah*mee/). Believers in Shinto worship the kami of mountains, rivers, rocks, and trees. They believe that heavenly

Mount Fuji, Japan's tallest mountain, is a sacred place in the Shinto religion.

bodies have life. The sun is the golden goddess Amaterasu, and the moon is her silvery brother Tsukiyomi (/soo*kee*yoh*mee/).

The Shinto religion is based on ceremonies rather than rules. No one person is named as its founder. Its ancient beliefs have no sacred book or "bible." The faith did not even have a name until the Chinese labeled it Shinto. The name means "way of the gods" and was first used in the 500s to distinguish the native Japanese religion from Buddhism.

Shinto focuses both on the gentle, beautiful aspects of nature as well as on the fierce occurrences such as earthquakes, **typhoons**, and volcanoes. For example, one of the kami might be found in an oddly twisted tree, an unusual insect, or a wise old man. Have you ever felt a sense of awe when viewing a full white moon or a red maple leaf? Someone who follows Shinto would say such feelings are inspired by kami.

> ## Vocabulary
>
> **typhoon,** n. a windy storm with heavy rain; a hurricane
>
> **shrine,** n. a place considered holy because it is associated with a holy person or event
>
> **ritual,** n. an act or series of actions done in the same way in a certain situation, such as a religious ceremony

Shinto followers worship their gods at **shrines**. These holy places are usually surrounded by sacred trees and have flowing water nearby. **Rituals** begin with washing ceremonies. You may have heard the saying "cleanliness is next to godliness." According to Shinto, one must be clean in the presence of spirits.

Shinto shrines were built to worship kami, or Japanese nature spirits.

Millions of Japanese practice Shinto today. They worship in their homes, at small roadside shrines, and at larger temples and gardens. They recite prayers and offer gifts of cakes, flowers, and money to the kami.

Buddhism: The Open Mind

Imagine yourself standing before a Buddhist master. He asks you a question and tells you that by answering you will better understand the ways of the Buddha. The master says, "You have climbed to the top of a ten-foot pole. How can you climb the rest of the way?"

How would you answer that question? Would you think that no one can climb higher than the top? If so, the Buddhist master would probably suggest that you meditate. That is, sit quietly and open your mind to all possibilities.

To understand the master's advice, it will help to learn a little about the founder of Buddhism, Siddhartha Gautama (/sih*dar*tuh/ gow*tuh*muh/). He was a young prince who lived in India in the 500s BCE. He asked searching questions about life. Eventually, he became known as the Buddha, or the "Enlightened One."

One day while sitting and meditating for a long time under a giant fig tree, he believed he became "enlightened." He believed that he had gained knowledge of the true path in life. Gautama spent the rest of his life teaching others what he had learned.

Buddhism is based on the teachings of Siddhartha Gautama, who is called Buddha or the "Enlightened One."

The Buddha's followers carried his teachings from India to other parts of the world, including China, Korea, and Japan.

The Four Truths and the Eightfold Path

What were those thoughts about life that the Buddha had under the fig tree? In his first **sermon**, the Buddha spoke of Four Noble Truths. These Truths are the foundation of Buddhism.

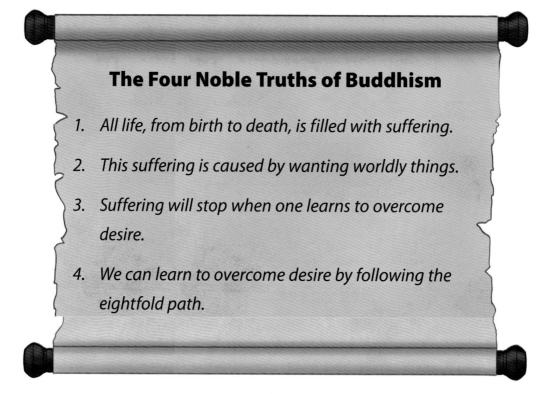

The Four Noble Truths of Buddhism

1. *All life, from birth to death, is filled with suffering.*

2. *This suffering is caused by wanting worldly things.*

3. *Suffering will stop when one learns to overcome desire.*

4. *We can learn to overcome desire by following the eightfold path.*

You probably noticed that the fourth Truth refers to an "eightfold path" that a person should follow. According to Buddha, there are eight things that one must do to achieve enlightenment. A person has achieved enlightenment when he or she has no desire or suffering.

The **dharma wheel** is the symbol for this eightfold path. By getting rid of greed, anger, and fear, people can gain happiness and **serenity** and eventually achieve enlightenment.

Steps in the Eightfold Path

Right Understanding (understanding Buddha's teachings)

Right Thought (thinking kind thoughts)

Right Speech (not telling lies or using angry words)

Right Action (not harming any person or animal)

Right Work (doing jobs that help others and makes no one suffer)

Right Effort (thinking before you act)

Right Mindfulness (being alert and aware)

Right Meditation (gaining a calm and focused mind)

Each spoke on this Buddhist dharma wheel stands for one of the eight "right" things.

Buddhism took root in Japan after 500 CE. Different groups tried to understand exactly what the Buddha had meant when he talked about achieving enlightenment. Some believed that the ideal of Buddhism was to follow the Buddha's focus on meditation. Other groups believed that the Buddha also wanted people to stay in touch with the world and help others follow the right path.

Zen Buddhism followed the second school of thought. Zen masters focus on teaching their students the *way* to peace. Zen does teach that people can find happiness through meditation, but it also teaches that through doing orderly tasks people can find happiness. These tasks include ordinary daily work, the ritual tea ceremony, and even **martial arts**. Therefore, Zen Buddhism focuses on both discipline and meditation.

Do you remember the question about climbing above the top of the pole? It was a Zen master who encouraged students to open their minds. What he meant was that Buddhists should allow their *minds* to climb higher than the top of the pole. That is, even if clearly their *bodies* could go no farther, their minds could. Zen Buddhist teachers today still encourage their students to meditate and let their minds go beyond the limits of normal thought. Zen teachers help people to open their minds to all possibilities. For a Zen Buddhist, "climbing above the pole" means giving the mind freedom to rise above the things of this world and reach true understanding.

Shinto and Buddhism

When Buddhism first arrived in Japan, some Japanese saw the new religion as a threat to Shinto. In time, however, most people began to look at things differently. They came to see that Buddhism was not a replacement for Shinto, nor was it a rival religion. They grew to see Buddhism as an addition that completes their religious beliefs. Many followers of Shinto began to embrace Buddhism without giving up their older ideas. Both Shinto and Buddhism live on, side by side in modern Japan. Many Japanese men and women who honor the kami at Shinto shrines also follow the mental discipline of Zen Buddhism.

Chapter 3
Japanese Feudalism

Rise of Feudal Japan You may have learned about feudalism when you studied the European Middle Ages. Feudalism is a system of government in which land is exchanged for loyalty and services. Under feudalism, people were born with a permanent position in society.

The Big Question

In what ways was a shogun more powerful than an emperor?

Vocabulary

lotus, n. a water lily, considered sacred in parts of Asia

By 800 CE, the descendants of the Yamato clan were firmly established as the rulers of Japan. They built a splendid palace in the present-day city of Kyoto, where emperors would continue to live for more than one thousand years. Safe inside the palace walls, these rulers of Japan strolled in gardens where golden sunbeams sparkled on **lotus** pools. They dressed in silks and drank ceremonial tea.

Kyoto's Imperial Palace garden today.

Japanese emperors, such as Emperor Kanmu of the Yamato clan, became isolated inside their palace and gardens.

Outside the palace walls, however, life was very different. As the rich got richer, the poor got poorer. Ordinary people eventually grew tired of paying high taxes to support the fancy lifestyle of the court. Some began to refuse to pay their taxes. Others moved away from the emperor's court and placed themselves under the protection of wealthy landowners. These changes decreased the emperor's tax income and increased the power of the landowners.

This painting shows a samurai on horseback. The samurai were fierce warriors.

Over time, more and more peasants sought protection from landowners. The landowners began to exert more and more influence over political affairs. Landowners also began to build up private armies of

> **Vocabulary**
>
> **samurai,** n. in feudal Japan, a Japanese warrior; the plural form is also samurai.

warriors known as **samurai** (/sah*muh*rye/). Soon the landowners became warlords, and eventually, the warlords began to struggle with one another.

Yoritomo and the Rise of Shoguns

After many years of conflict, a warlord named Yoritomo (/yor*ee*toh*mo/) rose to the top. Yoritomo's march to power began when a rival warlord executed many of his family members, including his parents. Yoritomo swore he would get revenge.

Yoritomo and his brother established an army, with Yoritomo's brother as general. At first, only three hundred samurai marched behind them, but eventually, there were more than twenty thousand. The army won battle after battle, and Yoritomo gained military control of the country.

Yoritomo now held power, but he was worried. His followers had sworn loyalty to him, but they had also followed his brother into battle. Yoritomo saw his brother as a threat and sent soldiers after him. Eventually, Yoritomo's brother was forced to kill himself.

Yoritomo became Japan's first shogun.

In 1192, the emperor declared that Yoritomo was the supreme military commander, or **shogun** (/shoh*gun/). Yoritomo continued to honor the emperor, but a lot of power had shifted from the emperor to the shogun. The emperor was now nothing more than a **figurehead**, an honored symbol of the empire. The shogun had all the military power, and he soon began making all the political decisions as well. This was the beginning of the feudal period in Japanese history.

Japanese Feudalism

During the European Middle Ages, a king granted land to a lord. The lord, in return, swore loyalty to the king and agreed to fight in the king's army. Then the lord made similar land grants to his own **vassals**, or knights, who agreed to serve the lord. Below the knights were the peasants, or serfs, who worked the land. Thus, society was like a pyramid, with the king on top. Peasants, **artisans**, and merchants were at the bottom of the social order.

In Japan, the concept was the same, but the system had some differences. The top man under the emperor was the shogun. Below him were regional warlords known as daimyo (/dime*yoh/). After that came the samurai warriors. Ordinary people—peasants, artisans, and merchants—were on the bottom rungs of the ladder.

Japan's Feudal Society

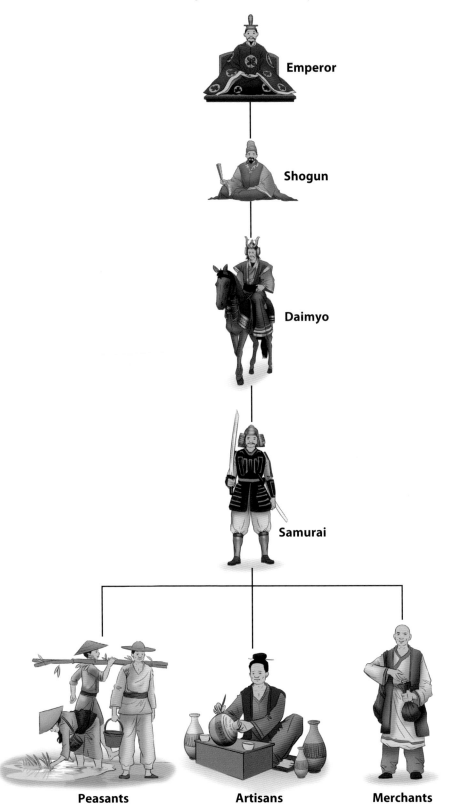

Emperor

Shogun

Daimyo

Samurai

Peasants

Artisans

Merchants

The Japanese empire was big, and the shoguns put the daimyo in charge of large pieces of land. In return, the daimyo pledged their loyalty to the shogun and promised him the support of their armies. The daimyo then built strong forces of samurai warriors.

The samurai pledged loyalty and service but not to the central government. Instead, they were loyal to their local lords, the daimyo. Indeed, the word *samurai* means "those who serve." The samurai swore to serve and protect their lords—or die trying.

The long period of shogun rule, which lasted from the late 1100s to the late 1800s, was also the great age of the samurai. In many ways, these samurai warriors were like the medieval knights of Europe. They were professional fighters who served their lords, and they lived in accordance with a demanding code of behavior.

The Story of a Samurai

In order to get an idea of how the samurai lived, let's look at the life of an imaginary young samurai named Katsu. Katsu was born to be a samurai. He was the son of a samurai, and his sons would be samurai, too. As soon as Katsu could talk, his father began teaching him what it meant to be a samurai. He told him about **Bushido** (/boo*shih*doh/), or the way of the warrior. This code of values guided every samurai's life and would guide Katsu.

> **Vocabulary**
>
> **Bushido,** n. literally, "the way of the warrior"; in feudal Japan, a code of values by which the samurai lived

"Honor, bravery, and loyalty, my son," instructed Katsu's father. "These come before all else. This is the code by which you shall live your life." On his fifth birthday, the boy received his first sword. Now he was a samurai.

Indeed, being a samurai was something to be proud of. Only about five percent of the people in all the empire were samurai. Other than the shogun or daimyo, only a samurai could wear a sword.

Katsu's family lived in a large house near the families of other samurai. His father served the daimyo, who lived in a strong central castle. Around the daimyo and samurai lived artisans, merchants, and peasants. The daimyo, the samurai, and the ordinary people inhabited three separate worlds, and a person living in one of them would never even dream of living in any other.

Katsu's father had faced death on the battlefield many times. But it was peacetime now. The ruling shogun was firmly in power, and there was no threat of civil war. Katsu's father served the daimyo by overseeing the daimyo's many peasant villages.

A samurai took all of his tasks very seriously. For Katsu's father to fall short in his duties would bring disgrace on him and his whole family. Disgrace was a serious matter. A samurai who failed to serve honorably and loyally was expected to commit seppuku (/seh*poo*koo/)—to take his own life.

Because he was born to be a samurai, Katsu had much to learn. He learned to read and write, and he became an expert in fencing, wrestling, horseback riding, and archery.

Studying the ways of Zen Buddhism, he learned to calm his mind and racing heart, and to consider all possibilities before taking action. Katsu and other warriors learned to balance the Zen traditions of serenity and kindness toward all creatures with samurai fierceness.

Hundreds of tiny scales make up this samurai's armor. This design gave the warrior flexibility, as well as protection.

Most importantly, Katsu learned to face hardship and death without fear. To harden himself to suffering, he walked barefoot in the winter's snow. He went without food for days and worked in the blistering summer sun until he felt faint.

Between the ages of thirteen and fifteen, a samurai officially became an adult. He took part in a special coming-of-age ceremony and received a suit of armor. He began tying his hair in a topknot. From this ceremony on, a samurai carried two swords. The first, a long sword, was his battle weapon, to be used to kill others. If Katsu ever failed to serve his daimyo loyally, if he ever faced disgrace or dishonor, he would use his second sword, a short sword, to end his own life.

As Katsu grew to manhood, he came to recognize the serious role he'd been born into. As a samurai, he was more than a well-trained soldier. He was a protector of all that was right and honorable. He was always ready to defend his lord and protect the feudal way of life.

Chapter 4
Everyday Life and Arts

The Townspeople The daimyo lived in a castle, surrounded by a "castle town." High-ranking samurai lived closest to the daimyo; farther out were the dwellings of lesser samurai, and then those of artisans, merchants, and priests. Scattered through the nearby countryside were peasant villages. What was daily life like for ordinary people?

The Big Question

How did daily life differ based on people's place in society?

Townspeople—the artisans and merchants—wore clothes made of coarse linen and cotton rather than the bright silks of the upper classes. Their daimyo did not allow them to build big houses or to use gold or silver for decoration. Their children did not go to school, as young samurai did. Instead, they went to work.

The artisans ranked higher on the social ladder than the merchants. The upper classes thought that the merchants were the lowest type of people because they produced nothing but instead bought and sold what other people made. Members of the upper classes also looked down on merchants because they handled money. This was something noblemen did not do. Ideally, a samurai never handled money himself. He had servants to perform such tasks.

In this painting, a daimyo on horseback looks at his castle.

The artisans had to follow strict rules. A baker might take great pride in his profession; probably he was descended from a long line of bakers. Nevertheless, the baker would never go to where the samurai lived without an invitation. If he had to deliver a cake to a samurai house, he would do so modestly and quietly, and he would be sure to remove his wooden clogs before stepping into the samurai's house.

The Peasants

On the edge of town were temples, shrines, and burial grounds. Beyond those areas were the farmlands, a checkerboard of **rice paddies** interrupted here and there by tiny villages where peasants usually lived.

The seasons directed a peasant's life. There was the planting time when men, women, and children pushed rice seedlings into the knee-deep mud. There were long days of harvest when they hurried to bring in crops before the heavy rains.

The peasants did backbreaking labor, but their work was important. After all, the rice they grew was the source of the daimyo's wealth.

Arts and Entertainment

There was one activity that brought pleasure to the townspeople but was considered too common for the samurai. Several times each year, traveling **Kabuki** (/kuh*book*kee/) players probably came to town.

> ## Vocabulary
>
> **rice paddy,** n. a field that is flooded to grow rice
>
> **Kabuki,** n. popular, traditional Japanese dramas with singing and dancing

The wealth of a daimyo was measured by how much rice his peasants could grow.

Even today, a Kabuki player appears in colorful costume and distinct makeup.

Performance day had to be sunny because the theater had no roof. Performers in colorful costumes exaggerated their movements and wore heavy makeup. Filling the stage, they sang, danced, and acted out stories of love, war, and heroism.

Sometimes the spectators joined the actors on the stage. It was a noisy, lively affair. Tea and food vendors squeezed through the audience. The snacks they sold were in great demand because a performance could last up to eighteen hours.

An earlier form of drama, the Noh theater was seen as more fitting for the upper classes. In contrast to Kabuki, a Noh play had little action. Two actors wearing carved masks performed on a bare wooden stage. Meanwhile, a chorus of men chanted about ideals such as unselfishness and honor. The only scenery was a single screen painted with a pine tree. This served as a reminder that Noh plays were originally performed at Shinto shrines, often in front of sacred trees.

Some high-ranking daimyo, or lords, had Noh stages built at their own castles. In several ways, the actors were a lot like the samurai themselves. The all-male Noh casts were very physically fit. The actors were well-trained and highly disciplined. Before each show they spent time in a special "mirror room," where they meditated and focused their minds on their performance.

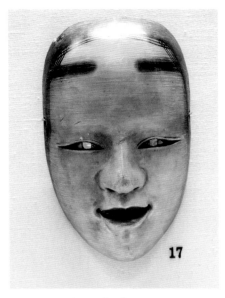

This is a Noh mask of a young woman.

The Flow of Life in Three Lines

By now, you probably picture feudal Japan as a warrior's world, and in many ways it was. But there was one samurai who became famous by using his pen rather than his sword. Taking the name of Basho, this young samurai became a master of a poetry form called **haiku** (/hye*koo/). In just three written lines, Basho could create a picture, reflect a feeling, or capture the meaning of life. For centuries, other haiku artists took inspiration from him.

Basho was the pen name used by Matsuo Munefusa, a samurai who lived in the 1600s and wrote haiku.

The Japanese nobility had enjoyed poetry since the early days of the empire. Because haiku was short and simple, everyone could understand and appreciate it.

Haiku spoke of nature—a part of everyone's experience. It would become one of the world's most popular poetry forms. Sometimes funny and sometimes sad, haiku captures the flow of everyday life. As you end this chapter, let yourself imagine what this poet of Japan saw and felt more than three hundred years ago:

Spider, say again!

It's so hard to hear your voice

in the autumn wind.

—Basho

Chapter 5
Changes Come to Japan

The Mongols A peaceful, prosperous life for the townspeople and peasants depended on how well the local daimyo and samurai could defend their territory. But there were also times when Japan had to defend itself against outside invaders.

The Big Question

How did foreign trade bring about the end of the shogun era?

One of the most powerful military forces the world has ever seen were the great Mongol armies of the 1100s and the 1200s. The Mongols created an empire that stretched from China to eastern Europe. The Mongol ruler Kublai Khan, grandson of the great conqueror Chinggis Khan, set his sights on Japan in the late 1200s.

In 1268, Kublai Khan sent a letter to Japan's capital. He threatened to attack if the Japanese did not agree to pay him money to keep peace. Both the emperor and the shogun ignored the threats.

Kublai Khan launched an invasion of Japan from Korea. The first attack came in 1274 when a fleet of nine hundred ships arrived on the shores of the empire's southernmost island, Kyushu.

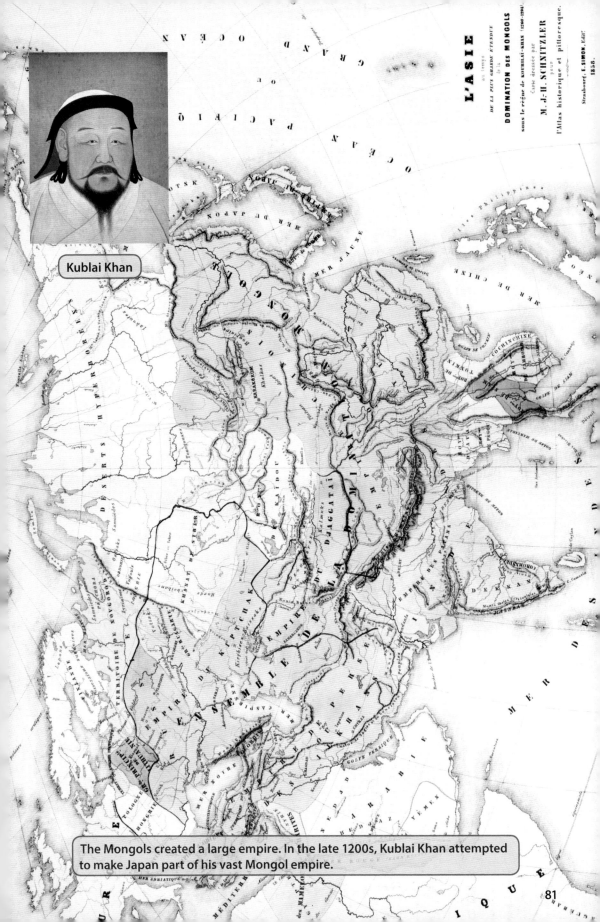

Kublai Khan

The Mongols created a large empire. In the late 1200s, Kublai Khan attempted to make Japan part of his vast Mongol empire.

The Mongols first tried to invade Japan in 1274.

On the first day of battle, the Mongol invaders were victorious, and they returned to their ships that night. It was a deadly mistake. A storm blew in, splintering the invaders' vessels and killing one third of their troops. The invasion failed.

A much larger attack came in 1281. This time, two separate armies joined in the assault on Hakata Bay. About forty thousand Mongol, Korean, and northern Chinese troops met up with another one hundred thousand troops from southern China. Some 4,400

Mongol warships arrived on the shores of Kyushu. Kublai Khan meant business.

Before the invaders could launch their attack, another storm blew in. This time it packed the fury of a full-scale typhoon, destroying most of the attacking ships and nearly half of the Mongol forces. Once again, the remaining Mongol invaders went home in defeat.

The Japanese did not believe that these storms were accidents or coincidences. They believed that each of these two storms was an example of kamikaze (/kah*mih*kah*zee/), meaning divine wind. The gods, wanting to protect Japan, had sent these divine winds to defeat the Mongol invasions.

The Japanese believe kamikaze, or divine winds, saved them from two Mongol invasions.

The Europeans Arrive

Almost three hundred years later, a different kind of threat reached Japan. In September 1543, an unusual ship appeared off the shore of one of Japan's smaller islands. It carried newcomers who came to trade. They brought one item unlike anything the Japanese had ever seen. According to one account, it caused an explosion like lightning and a noise like thunder.

The remarkable object was a **musket**, and the strangers who brought it sailed from Portugal. The Portuguese had already explored the coasts of Africa and Asia, as well as many of the islands of the Pacific. Now they had come to Japan, bringing the musket—a firearm that would change Japanese warfare forever.

Japan at first welcomed the Western traders. After the Portuguese vessels, Spanish, Dutch, and English trade ships also arrived. Japan's daimyo were intrigued by Western ideas. They were also eager to obtain firearms. Over the centuries, the daimyo had spent many years fighting among themselves, struggling to determine who would be the shogun. The musket soon became an important weapon in these struggles. After the arrival of the Europeans, no daimyo could hope to become shogun unless an army of musketeers backed him.

The Portuguese brought muskets to Japan.

Along with the Western traders came **missionaries**. A Catholic group, the **Jesuits**, hoped to set up permanent missions in Japan. On the west coast of Kyushu, a local warlord offered the Jesuits harborside land in the little fishing village of Nagasaki (/nah*guh*sah*kee/). In time, this village would become the chief city on Kyushu.

For twenty-five years, the Westerners—both traders and missionaries—enjoyed a welcome in Japan. The technology and ideas they introduced would greatly influence the course of Japanese history.

The arrival of European traders and missionaries in the 1500s introduced new weapons and the Christian religion to Japan.

A Closed World

In 1603, the Tokugawa (/toh*koo*gah*wuh/) family of shoguns gained control of Japan and ruled from the city of Edo, which is now Tokyo. Earlier shoguns had welcomed Western trade and ideas. Now, the Tokugawa removed the welcome mat, banning all foreign missionaries from Japan. This was done largely because Christian teachings challenged traditional Japanese ideas and beliefs. Also, the governing powers of various Christian churches were not within the control of the ruling shogun. The ruling shogun ordered that no Japanese would be permitted to practice Christianity. He even used torture and execution to persuade people to abandon the religion.

Still, the missionaries and priests kept coming, along with foreign trade ships. The Japanese worried that foreign armies determined to turn Japan into a colony would follow these visitors. From 1600

The Tokugawa shoguns allowed the Dutch to have a trading post at Nagasaki. No other Europeans or Americans were allowed into Japan. In this image you can see the Dutch trading post.

to 1868, shoguns barred nearly all Westerners' ships from Japan's harbors. Only the Dutch could visit as they were mainly interested in trade, but even they were confined to one port near Nagasaki.

In 1636, the shogun issued an **exclusion** order. The order prevented Japanese people from traveling abroad and foreigners from coming in. In 1639, it became against the law to build a big, seagoing ship. The surrounding seas helped the shoguns isolate their people, although Japan continued to trade with its Asian neighbors.

Under the Tokugawa shoguns, Japan would remain a **secluded**, or closed, world for more than two hundred years.

Opening Doors

In the late 1700s, Japan was still maintaining its "exclusion" policy, banning trade with all Westerners except the Dutch. However, three nations—Russia, Britain, and the United States—began to knock loudly on its doors.

In the early 1700s, Russia's ruler Peter the Great asked that Russian ships be allowed to stop at Japanese ports for supplies. Peter died before setting up trade relations with Japan, but in the late 1700s, Catherine the Great tried again. Czarina Catherine tried to force the shogun to open his ports, but the Russian strong-arm methods backfired. Japan closed its doors more tightly. The shogun ordered that any foreign vessel that came close to his shores be destroyed.

Meanwhile, Britain had forced trade agreements with China. The shogun's fears increased. He worried that Japan, too, would be forced to welcome foreign ships.

He was right to worry. In July 1853, four black-hulled American vessels steamed into Tokyo Bay. A stern-faced United States naval officer, Commodore Matthew Perry, came before the shogun. Perry presented a letter from the president of the United States. It demanded that Japan open its ports to trade.

Commodore Matthew Perry arrived in Tokyo Bay in 1853. His visit helped open trade relations between Japan and the United States.

Perry soon made a second visit—this time bringing four extra warships. The American show of force did the trick. The shogun and his advisers knew that they could not stand up against the United States Navy. They signed a **trade treaty** with the United States.

This first treaty turned out to be only the beginning. After agreeing to trade with the United States, how could the shogun refuse other nations? Britain, France, and Russia soon demanded and won trade rights, too. Suddenly, Japan was bustling with foreign traders.

The End of Shogun Rule

After several years of foreign trade, some Japanese grew unhappy with the arrangement. They thought that the foreigners had been given special privileges, and they blamed the shogun for allowing this to happen. Many Japanese complained about their lives under the shogun. Merchants, although making plenty of money, remained near the bottom of the social ladder. Peasants paid heavy taxes. The samurai, who were much less important than before because of the growing importance of trade, were discontented. The daimyo grumbled about being forced to maintain expensive houses in the capital.

Eventually, a rebellion against the shogun broke out. Where did the rebels look for the solution to their problems? They looked to the emperor. Remember, although shoguns ruled the land, an emperor still served as a royal figurehead. "Honor the emperor!" became the rebels' cry.

In 1867, the shogun stepped down and in 1868, a new government was formed. The emperor was restored to the role of official head of state. Shinto was once again declared the **state religion.** The Shinto religion reminded people that their emperor ruled as a descendant of the sun goddess Amaterasu.

This was not, however, a return to the old days when the emperor ran the affairs of state. A new government conducted business in the name of the emperor.

The end of shogun rule marked the end of Japan's feudal age. The new government announced that rank in Japanese society now included consideration of how much a person knew of Western science and practical affairs. The old system of inherited rank— samurai, peasants, artisans, and merchants—was abolished. Japanese of all ranks were equal under the law. Samurai could buy and sell goods, and artisans, merchants, and peasants could serve in Japan's new modern army.

The Japanese adopted a new attitude about the world they shared. Remember when the shoguns closed Japan's doors to Westerners and did not allow its people to leave their home shores? In contrast, the new government stated that "knowledge shall be sought throughout the world."

The Japanese began to visit the United States and Europe. They studied Western science and shook off their longtime dislike for trade and commerce. Japan built a mighty naval fleet. The Land of the Rising Sun prepared to take a powerful place in world affairs.

Japan's last shogun was removed from power in 1867.

Glossary

A

archipelago, n. a chain of islands (46)

aristocrat, n. a person of the upper or noble class whose status is usually inherited (50)

artisan, n. a person with a certain skill in making things (66)

B

Buddhism, n. a religion that began in India and is based on the teachings of Siddhartha Gautama (48)

Bushido, n. literally, "the way of the warrior"; in feudal Japan, a code of values by which the samurai lived (68)

C

clan, n. a group of families claiming a common ancestor (46)

D

dharma wheel, n. the symbol of Buddhism. The eight spokes of the wheel symbolize the eightfold path. (59)

E

exclusion, n. the state of being shut out or kept out of a group or agreement (87)

F

figurehead, n. a person who leads or rules in name only but actually has no power (66)

G

gangplank, n. a small movable bridge used to get on and off a ship (48)

H

haiku, n. a form of poetry having seventeen syllables in three lines (77)

I

isolation, n. separation from others (46)

J

Jesuit, n. a member of the Catholic religious group called the Society of Jesus (85)

K

Kabuki, n. popular, traditional Japanese dramas with singing and dancing (74)

L

lotus, n. a water lily, considered sacred in parts of Asia (62)

M

martial arts, n. any of several arts of self-defense, such as karate and judo, that are widely practiced as a sport (61)

missionary, n. a person on a journey for the purpose of spreading a particular religious belief (85)

musket, n. a type of muzzle-loading gun that was used before the invention of the rifle (84)

P

Pacific Rim, n. a term used to describe nations that border the Pacific Ocean (44)

R

rice paddy, n. a field that is flooded to grow rice (74)

ritual, n. an act or series of actions done in the same way in a certain situation, such as a religious ceremony (54)

S

samurai, n. in feudal Japan, a Japanese warrior; the plural form is also samurai. (65)

secluded, adj. having little or no contact with others; isolated (87)

serenity, n. a feeling of calm and peacefulness (59)

sermon, n. a speech on a religious topic given by a religious leader (58)

Shinto, n. a Japanese religion in which people worship gods and spirits associated with nature (48)

shogun, n. a title meaning great general, given to the strongest military leader in feudal Japan (66)

shrine, n. a place considered holy because it is associated with a holy person or event (54)

silkworm, n. a caterpillar that produces silk, which is used to make thread or cloth (49)

spirit, n. an unseen life-giving force (52)

state religion, n. a religion established by law as the only official religion of a country (90)

T

tea ceremony, n. a way of preparing and presenting tea (49)

"trade treaty", (phrase) an international agreement of conditions of trade in goods and services (89)

typhoon, n. a windy storm with heavy rain; a hurricane (54)

V

vassal, n. a person who receives land from a ruler and in return promises to fight for that ruler (66)

Z

Zen Buddhism, n. a type of Buddhism developed in Japan that emphasizes meditation and thoughtful tasks as the way to peace (60)

Core Knowledge®

CKHG™
Core Knowledge HISTORY AND GEOGRAPHY™

Series Editor-In-Chief
E.D. Hirsch, Jr.

Editorial Directors
Linda Bevilacqua and Rosie McCormick

Early Russia

Subject Matter Expert

Matthew M. Davis, PhD, University of Virginia

Illustration and Photo Credits

Feudal Japan

Subject Matter Expert

Yongguang Hu, PhD, Department of History, James Madison University

Illustration and Photo Credits